There Goes the Water

A Song About the Water Cycle

by Laura Purdie Salas

illustrated by Sergio De Giorgi

Sing along to the tune of

𝄞 "Pop Goes the Weasel."

Learn how Earth's water cycle works.

PICTURE WINDOW BOOKS
a capstone imprint

The audio file for this book is available for download at:
http://www.capstonekids.com/sciencesongs

Editor: Jill Kalz
Designers: Abbey Fitzgerald and Lori Bye
Art Director: Nathan Gassman
Production Specialist: Jane Klenk
The illustrations in this book were created digitally.

Picture Window Books
151 Good Counsel Drive, P.O. Box 669
Mankato, MN 56002-0669
877-845-8392
www.picturewindowbooks.com

Printed in the United States of America in North Mankato, Minnesota.
092009
005618CGS10

Library of Congress Cataloging-in-Publication Data
Salas, Laura Purdie.
There goes the water : a song about the water cycle /
by Laura Purdie Salas, illustrated by Sergio De Giorgi.
p. cm. — (Science songs)
Includes index.
ISBN 978-1-4048-5766-7 (library binding)
1. Hydrologic cycle—Juvenile literature. I. Title.
GB848.S25 2010
551.48—dc22
                          2009033381

Thanks to our advisers for their expertise, research, and advice:

Jerald Dosch, Ph.D., Visiting Assistant Professor of Biology
Macalester College

Terry Flaherty, Ph.D., Professor of English
Minnesota State University, Mankato

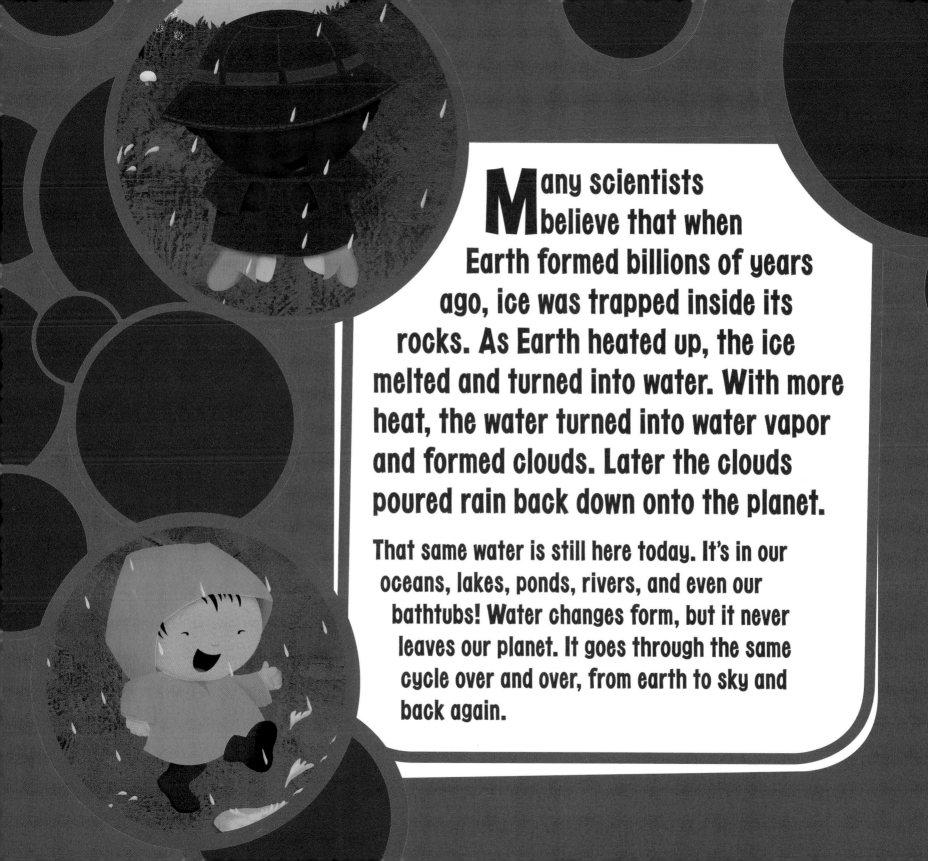

Many scientists believe that when Earth formed billions of years ago, ice was trapped inside its rocks. As Earth heated up, the ice melted and turned into water. With more heat, the water turned into water vapor and formed clouds. Later the clouds poured rain back down onto the planet.

That same water is still here today. It's in our oceans, lakes, ponds, rivers, and even our bathtubs! Water changes form, but it never leaves our planet. It goes through the same cycle over and over, from earth to sky and back again.

Water covers most of the earth

In puddle, lake, and ocean.

It goes from ground to sky and back down:

Never-ending motion!

4

Water takes many forms. It can be solid ice. It can be liquid water. And it can be gas, which is the water vapor that forms clouds.

5

Water trickled down through the rocks

Way back when Earth was forming.

Today that water falls from the sky

When it is storming.

Our water has been many places. The water you drank this morning might have been part of a surfer's wave 50 years ago. A drop in a river might have been a snowflake in a blizzard 1,000 years ago.

Tiny creeks and great rivers flow

In salty seas' direction.

8

Most flowing water goes toward the oceans. Tiny creeks flow into streams. Streams flow into rivers. Many rivers empty into the oceans. This cycle keeps our oceans full.

9

This is where the cycle begins—

Stage One: Collection!

Wind and sun pull water toward sky,

Its airy destination.

It turns into invisible gas—

Evaporation!

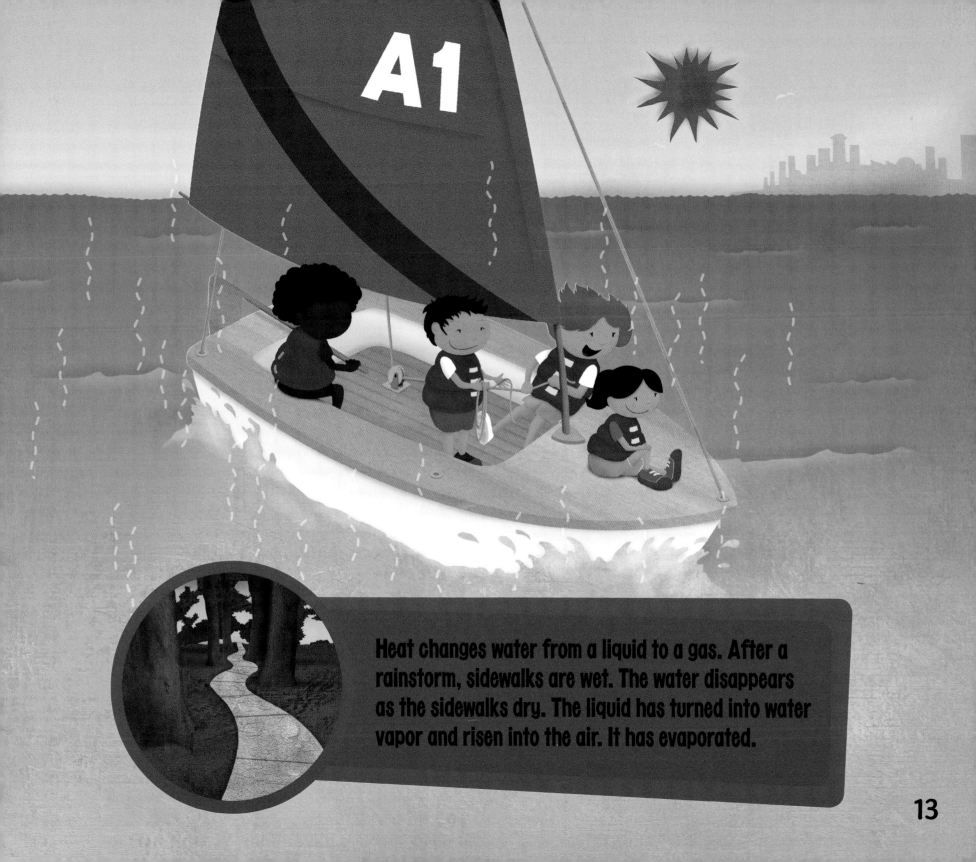

Heat changes water from a liquid to a gas. After a rainstorm, sidewalks are wet. The water disappears as the sidewalks dry. The liquid has turned into water vapor and risen into the air. It has evaporated.

Now the gas turns liquid again.

It's time for cloud formation.

Each droplet covers one piece of dust.

That's condensation!

As water vapor rises, it can attach to tiny pieces of dust in the air. Then the gas turns back into liquid. It makes a water drop. That's called condensation. Clouds are full of tiny droplets of water.

Heavy clouds drop rain to the ground.

It's called precipitation.

Rain is not the only kind of precipitation. Hail and snow are other kinds. Hail is ice that falls from clouds. It can be as small as a pea or as large as a softball!

19

The water cycle circles around—

Great transformation!

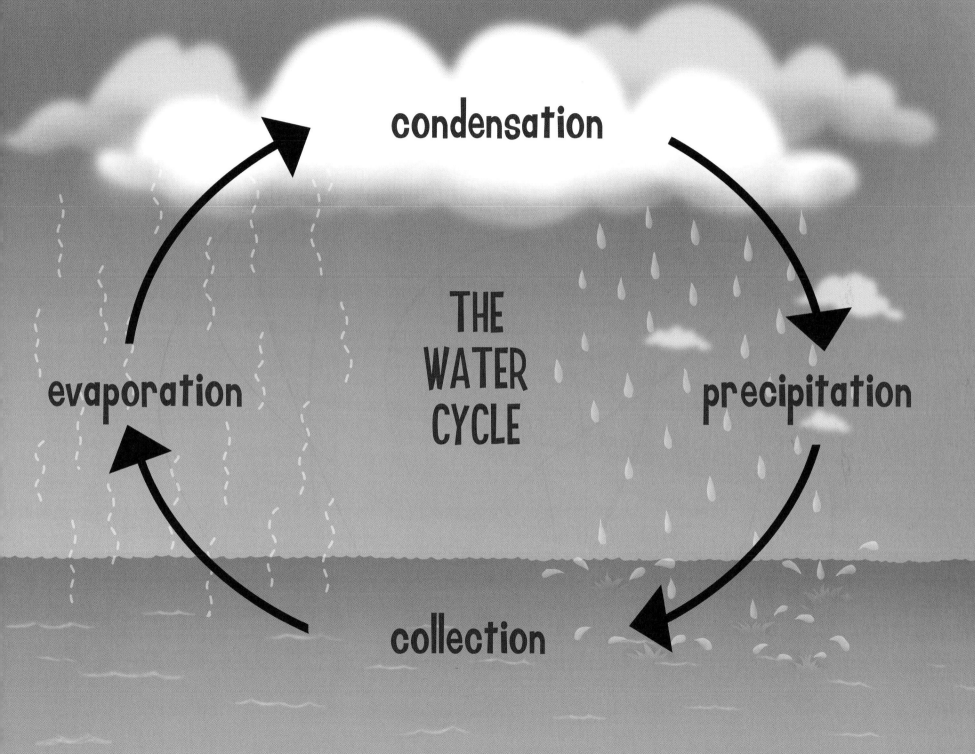

condensation

evaporation

THE
WATER
CYCLE

precipitation

collection

There Goes the Water

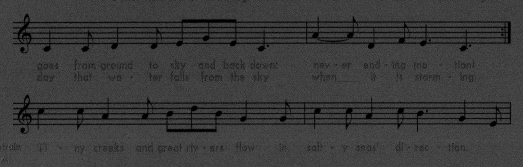

1. Wa - ter cov-ers most of the earth in pud - dle, lake, and o - cean. It
2. Wa - ter trick-led down through the rocks way back when earth was form - ing. To -

goes from ground to sky and back down; nev - er end - ing mo - tion!
day that wa - ter falls from the sky when it is storm - ing.

Refrain Ti - ny creeks and great riv - ers flow in salt - y seas' di - rec - tion.

This is where the cy - cle be - gins — stage one: col - lec - tion!

3. Wind and sun pull water toward sky,
It's sky destination.
It turns into invisible gas—
Evaporation!

4. Now the gas turns liquid again,
It's time for cloud formation.
Each droplet covers one piece of dust,
That's condensation!

Refrain 2: Heavy clouds drop rain to the ground.
It's called precipitation.
The water cycle circles around—
Great transformation!

The audio file for this book is available for download at:
http://www.capstonekids.com/sciencesongs

Did You Know?

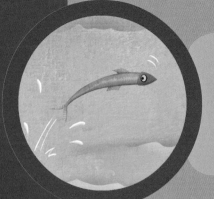

About **75** percent of Earth is covered with water. More than **97** percent of that water is salty. That means less than **3** percent of Earth's water is fresh water. About half of all fresh water is frozen in glaciers and polar ice caps.

Without water, nothing can live. Every plant and animal on Earth needs water.

We clean water before we drink it. We filter it to remove tiny pieces of dirt and minerals. We often add chemicals to water to kill germs.

The average person in the United States uses **80** to **100** gallons (**304** to **380** liters) of water each day.

Glossary

collection—water flowing toward the sea and gathering in a large body, such as a lake

condensation—changing from a gas to a liquid

cycle—a set of events that happen over and over again

evaporation—changing from a liquid to a gas

glacier—a large, slow-moving body of ice

polar ice cap—a huge body of ice at a planet's north or south pole

precipitation—water that falls from the clouds in the form of rain, hail, or snow

transformation—the changing from one form into another

water vapor—water in a gas form

To Learn More

More Books to Read

Green, Jen. *How the Water Cycle Works.* New York: PowerKids Press, 2008.

Jango-Cohen, Judith. *Why Does It Rain?* Minneapolis: Millbrook Press, 2006.

Morrison, Gordon. *A Drop of Water.* Boston: Houghton Mifflin, 2006.

Internet Sites

FactHound offers a safe, fun way to find Internet sites related to this book.
All of the sites on FactHound have been researched by our staff.

Here's all you do:

Visit www.facthound.com

FactHound will fetch the best sites for you!

Index

Look for all of the books in the Science Songs series:

Are You Living?
A Song About Living and Nonliving Things

Eight Great Planets!
A Song About the Planets

From Beginning to End:
A Song About Life Cycles

Home on the Earth:
A Song About Earth's Layers

I'm Exploring with My Senses:
A Song About the Five Senses

Many Creatures:
A Song About Animal Classifications

Move It! Work It!
A Song About Simple Machines

There Goes the Water:
A Song About the Water Cycle